Roy Fisher

A FURNACE

Edited by

Peter Robinson

Flood Editions

Chicago

Poetry copyright © 1986, 1988,
1994, 1996, 2005 by Roy Fisher
Introduction and editorial matter
copyright © 2018 by Peter Robinson
Published in the U.S.A. by Flood Editions
in 2018 under license from Bloodaxe Books, Ltd.,
which first published *The Long and the
Short of It: Poems 1955-2005* in 2005.
ISBN 978-0-9981695-5-2
Design and composition by Quemadura
Printed on acid-free, recycled paper
in the United States of America
First Edition

Contents

Introduction

Before his death on 21 March 2017, Roy Fisher discussed this new, stand-alone edition of *A Furnace*, for which agreements had been reached between Bloodaxe Books and Flood Editions. He had reluctantly accepted that he would write a fresh preface or afterword, though each time we talked of it on the phone it appeared to grow shorter and shorter in his mind. Fisher's ideal—could it have been practicable—would have been for the poem to stand absolutely alone, without any apparatus whatsoever. He did, however, point me in the direction of exactly what he'd had in mind when describing *A Furnace*, in the preface he was asked to compose for the 1986 first edition, as 'an engine devised, like a cauldron, or a still, or a blast-furnace, to invoke and assist natural processes of change.' For the first of these similes he was thinking of the Gundestrup Cauldron, discovered in 1891 in the Rævemosen bog in Himmerland, northern Denmark, near the place after which it is named. This prehistoric silver vessel is elaborated around its sides with representations of animals and gods not associated with the people who placed it in the ground in that part of Jutland, suggesting it had been constructed elsewhere and presented as a gift. For Fisher, it offers a representative container, such as his poem would be, which could absorb anything, from wherever, transforming it with creative heat for greater human benefit.

Introducing Fisher's *Selected Poems*, published by Flood Editions in 2011, August Kleinzahler observes:

> His masterwork, *A Furnace*, was issued by Oxford in 1986. Again, it is recognizably Fisher but not at all like anything else he'd written. Dedicated to John Cowper Powys, who would seem at first glance an unlikely model for the poet, it is a thirty-five-page, 1300-plus-line composition in seven parts, an excavation of a site through time, conflating the local aluminium works, John Dee, the Neolithic spirit world, Great-Grandfather William, Adolphe Sax, modern Chicago, the transit of Augusta Treverorum to Trier, and old rocks of every description, all of it glued together with a very loose, homemade animism. It is Fisher's richest and most challenging poem.

A Furnace is indeed Fisher's most capacious construction, not least in the historical, geographical, and cultural scope of its conflated materials and allusions. While keyed to relations with his native Birmingham—where the 'Introit', dated 12 November 1958, finds its twenty-eight-year-old author figure travelling on a bus within the city—the authorial consciousness (about a quarter of a century older) draws upon memories of, for instance, a visit to Chicago made in 1976, intimate local knowledge of the Derbyshire Peak District where he had by then settled, the history of the city of Trier in Germany, of an ancient tumulus in Brittany, the settlement of Ampurias in Catalonia, the salvaging of the German High Seas Fleet from Scapa Flow—as well as recollections of his early years in Kentish Road, Handsworth, and much more besides.

Developed out of the flexibly topic-switching mode evolved for 'Wonders of Obligation' (1979), once beyond the narrated establishing shots in the single place of its 'Introit', *A Furnace* uses a collaging style to evoke disparate materials in an over-layering of multiple landscapes, such as are described here in notes towards the poem which survive in Fisher's archive:

> The material is this stretch of country and its inter-relationship with itself, its quantum-pluralism, and its function (because of that pluralism and not because it's rural merely) in balancing, or rendering comprehensible the earlier cowpat of Birmingham culture. And there's the major Powysian metaphor of the superimposition of two landscapes.

This references the dedicatee of *A Furnace*, and his phrase quoted in it: *'Landscape superimposed / upon landscape.'* Fisher's poem also demonstrates at its most sustained a newly won ability to speak out directly upon such matters as the power relations that created Birmingham, or the ways that death is structured and controlled by religious and civic authorities in a historically Christian culture.

Fisher's reiterated preference for keeping his counsel in publications of *A Furnace* contrasts, in dramatic fashion, with what was revealed, after his death, by the survival of its working drafts—from which the passage above is drawn. These are contained in two unlined 'University Series Manuscript Books', with blue hard covers (now faded) and (frayed) maroon bindings, made by Standford & Mann Ltd., Manufacturing Stationers, at 72-73 New Street, Birmingham. They appear to have survived from much earlier than the period in which they were eventually used—the first dated 18 July 1983, and the latter 29 April 1985. This second notebook has two further dates from 1994 and 2000 indicating when it was taken up again for planning some Odes, which appear not to have been written, and for work on 'The Dow Low Drop', which was eventually brought to completion. The first of the two contains plans for *A Furnace*, as well as observations, reflection on progress, and draft passages to be incorporated eventually into its sections. The second begins with a fair copy of a completed draft showing increasing amounts of revision in its later sections. The first of these notebooks in particular is a revelation.

Fisher had been awarded a grant by the Arts Council to support his poem's composition, and would set about writing *A Furnace* with a degree of planning and self-consciousness unusual for this artist. In earlier interviews he had explained his preference, when writing *The Ship's Orchestra* (1966), for an additive method in which each section is completed without any idea of where the work's next passage would come from. In some of the earlier notes warming up for work on his poem, Fisher writes that 'My unwillingness/inability to plan work needs to go in' and then adds: 'I'm planning this one.' And plan it he did. *A Furnace* has, in this light, a genealogical connection with Basil Bunting's *Briggflatts*, for Fisher's poem too has an abstract design—not unlike Bunting's seasonal peaks and troughs—though in this case a movement into a center and away from it, one designed with a linear sequence, as required of a poem, but also conceived as a double spiral, by which following the movement into the central 'Core' will also take you out of it. This too is in complex dialogue with what we know of this poet's expressed preferences, his not liking to set up a hierarchy or center which would operate as a source of authority for the work.

By page 17 of the first notebook, Fisher had not only developed and designed the double spiral, curving in and out, but he had started to reflect on its purpose in the planned work—as here in a paragraph from an entry dated 24 July 1983:

> The form is by now partly there in the spiral. *What I've got to do is cartoon, not illusionize.* Work (Brecht, Hockney) in the light of how people can perceive without telling lies about how things are. The formal work of this poem is to distinguish clearly, and heal, or treat or supersede, the disjuncture between our cosmology and our language. *Ethic.*

Such observations see him plainly taking into account, yet moving beyond, the kinds of skepticism about 'ethics' that had informed his short poem of a decade before called 'It Is Writing' (1974) which concludes: 'I mistrust the poem in its hour of success, / a thing capable of being / tempted by ethics into the wonderful.' Yet this note is still very much in accord with Fisher's characteristic tensions. On the one hand, he would not have his work readily absorbed by being crudely moralized. On the other, he refused to be driven from expressing an ethic and cultural value because these things could be used as reductive handles in the reviewing and literary-critical culture in which he was compelled to operate.

The dangers of having such a plan of work are also commented on, when Fisher encourages himself to let the poem emerge and not succumb to the in-filling that his planning might risk—as in this note dated 3 October 1983, written before actual composition had begun:

> I'm not too happy about this way of doing it. It tends towards filler, and the marshalling of filler, with the assumption that there's stuff lying about inert and that it can somehow be made to fit, put on parade and told to get on with its companions. I'd be better with a pluralistic set of systems each of which lives and generates material which lives within it but isn't closed to the others.

He is also reflective about the heterogeneity of the materials he is bringing together, and how they run the risk of being considered arbitrary. The composition of his long poem thus involved him in the reconsideration, and making manifest, of much that his earlier work had kept implicit and his statements in interviews had tended to abjure. As he notes in passing here: '*The Ship's Orchestra* is a hermetic work that couldn't know what it had encoded in it.' With *A Furnace*, Fisher had evidently decided that he could no longer pretend not to know what his work was about, and the result is a new directness that inflects a great deal of his subsequent writing. This poem is his watershed, marking the shift between the early to mid-career work, and the emergence of his later styles.

Among the most striking of the workbooks' articulations of purpose and procedure is this, dated 28 February 1984:

> There is a transcendental optimistic purpose in my work. *Sauve qui peut*—or rather, strike out for the right way of understanding; don't wait to carry the committee. Those who can see must. Those who hear the signals must show. This is part of a long biological process which may go this way and that many times. Within an individual life it's of the greatest urgency. Political corollary.

Over a decade later, in 'Roy Fisher on Roy Fisher', where he subjects *The Dow Low Drop: New and Selected Poems* (1996) to a critical work over in the third person, the poet would take the opportunity to spell out such a 'political corollary' and with special reference to his long poem: 'Fisher's political disposition is plain enough to see: it constantly breaks the surface of *A Furnace*, though never programmatically'. Then, as the poet writes of himself, 'I take him to be an anarchist who simply has no time whatever for hierarchical systems, monotheisms or state authority; or for capitalism, along with the absorbent, malleable selves it breeds.' Still, for him 'the world ruled by such rackets is nevertheless the only world, into which everybody's born already swimming or going under.'

The tension between those urgencies in 'an individual life' and this 'only world' work themselves through in Fisher's reflective practice. The poet, as could be expected from published comments elsewhere, is highly skeptical of biography as an organizing principle:

> *Time.* There's the double flow of what lives as innovation and what lives as primeval, seen subjectively. But materials are not at all ordered by the crass language of my biography: that is, any material I can remember or historically conjure is treated first as simultaneous. Didactic point being that English tense and time language becomes authoritative and disposes of the past, which then has to be recovered—un-disposed of. And the parcels of time I'm concerned with are infinitesimal. If I use biographical tense it's as if quoting a song.

Fisher's tongue-in-cheek view of this strategy, though, was to suggest a work whose ambitiousness came at a price. Again in 'Roy Fisher on Roy Fisher', he wrote that *A Fur-*

nace, 'for all its unconscious or unashamed solipsism,' is 'one of the most ambitious recent English poems I've read.' The poem's scope and reach depends upon the simultaneity of all he could remember or conjure, which naturally disconnects it from its usual moorings in narratives, chronologies, or physical geographies and so risks the charge that it only exists—in this form at least—in the poet's mind. Yet the eventual purpose of composition and realization in the poem's form is to make all of it real and really shareable with readers beyond any such limitations, however 'unconscious or unashamed'.

Once planned, the double-spiral shape of the poem was then imagined in what appear strongly subjective, if not quite biographical terms in this 18 February 1984 note:

> Prospectus and method. I go in, with my dual nature holding together, not divided or dismissive, on a fluid run of what's on my mind now. I go in towards the core, knowing it to be not Apocalypse but that dry heterogeneous chamber. I go towards the core knowing that death, the lore of the dead, comes out towards me in a ratio as I go in. I start with what's currently in flux and telling me these things, the crusts, the deposits, the things of my life stored and found, will break loose and come in in due course.

Fisher had thus evolved a means not only for articulating and inhabiting the materials that would go into his cauldron, but for generating the heat that would help them to emerge transformed. He was also aware of human impulses in his own life which would have to be set to work in the composition, as here in notes dated 27 May 1984, written while working on the 'Introit':

> Whereas within life love seems a demanding and cruel imposition, within love, art takes on those qualities. This at least releases feeling, and releases language. The poem has to be a romantic poem, or it's a muffled and stuffy mysticism. And if the unbalanced romanticism of my life can't be a liquid running in among the poem, then it has to be relegated to the status of embarrassing and unproductive deviancy. I'm not having *that*.

Fisher thus set a deeply recessed inner life to work at a process of material change, allowing readers in turn to envisage productive relations with the mass and weight of their own histories, memories of the world, and individual lives.

Drawing up lists of material that might be used in his poem's seven sections, Fisher noted down: 'The Tarmac at O'Hare. Walking to America.' Though these two phrases were not to find their way into *A Furnace*, an evocation of

Chicago did take its place in a sequence upon the apocalyptic Pandemonium-like experience of our cities at night, and, in doing so, Fisher suggests analogies between his birthplace and the home base of his American publisher:

> This age has a cold blackness of Hell
> in cities at night. London
> is filled with it. Chicago cradles it
> in ice-green glitter along
> the dark of the lake. Birmingham Sparkbrook,
> Birmingham centre, Birmingham Castle Vale
> hang in it as holograms.

Those two phrases, 'The Tarmac at O'Hare' and 'Walking to America', were underlined in pencil and arrowed to a remark dated 4 August 1985 that says: 'To use. *Odes.*' Though no such works with that generic title were written, another reference among his notes to what would become 'A Sign Illuminated' (1987) suggests this trawl for unused materials did prompt further poems—and 'The Tarmac at O'Hare' would eventually do so in the third part of 'Songs from the Camel's Coffin' (1997):

> startled
> on stepping down to the battered tarmac of O'Hare
> to discover that the air above it,

the entire medium of elsewhere,
wasn't as I'd guessed it would have to be, a heavy
yellowish fluid tending towards glass,
towards mica.

Not only is this new edition of *A Furnace* the first posthumous publication from Roy Fisher's extraordinarily original writings, it is an illuminated sign, if sign were needed, that his 'Walking to America' is very much still in progress and still heading over 'battered tarmac' towards its projected destination.

PETER ROBINSON

A Note on the Text

A Furnace exists in three separately printed texts, the first and last of which were certainly proofread by Roy Fisher. They are the original Oxford University Press edition of 1986, the text included in *The Dow Low Drop: New and Selected Poems* (Bloodaxe Books, 1996), and that included in *The Long and the Short of It: Poems 1955-2005* (Bloodaxe Books, 2005). The second of these was assembled at the time of Fisher's hospitalization in the aftermath of a stroke. I do not know to what extent he was able to oversee its production. Fisher did oversee the assembling of the 2005 Bloodaxe volume, but it suffers from a number of late-life proofreading oversights, making, all in all, the first edition the most reliable. There is, however, one authoritative correction to the Oxford text made in the 1996 reprint of 'III. Authorities' where the nonexistent *'eclos paroisseau'* is amended to *'eclos paroissial'*. Other discrepancies between Oxford and Bloodaxe mostly derive from ambiguities of layout caused by the latter's interpretation of the Oxford impagination, creating some rogue stanza breaks that have been carried over into later printings.

Here, for the first time, these ambiguities of textual disposition have been resolved by consulting the hand-written fair copy of the poem in the second of its two working notebooks, whose contents are described above in the Introduction. Bloodaxe does, however, correctly record the section break before the final three lines of 'VI. The Many', which had been lost over a page break in Oxford. Thus the text printed here is, I believe, the most accurate to date, being based on the first printing, but taking into account two qualitative improvements in Bloodaxe, while removing the unintended stanza breaks that had crept in at later stages, and adding a circumflex to the proper name 'Le Nôtre'.

The material in the Appendix takes its place between these covers according to the following rationales. 'They Come Home' is printed here with Fisher's explicit permission because a completed draft of it appears, untitled, as part of 'IV. Core' in the first of the working notebooks. It had been taken out by the time the fair copy was transcribed into the second notebook. The reason, according to the poet, is that its biographical source, the aftermath of the deaths of his second wife Joyce Holliday's parents, was too close and raw at the time of *A Furnace*'s completion. 'They Come Home' first appeared as a stand-alone poem in the Cambridge magazine *Numbers* 5 (1989), some four years after its composition. Its layout, with two kinds of separation between the parts, is preserved from the poem's first collection in *Birmingham River* (Oxford University Press, 1994).

Fisher's attitude to the author's 'Preface' published in the 1986 Oxford edition was that it had been composed at the publisher's request and did not form part of his intentions for the poem. It was not reprinted with *A Furnace* again during his lifetime. He did, however, agree to its being included in *An Easily Bewildered Child: Occasional Prose 1963-2013* (Shearsman Books, 2014). It is included here in the Appendix, along with the author's 'Notes' from the Oxford edition, which Fisher did have reprinted with the poem in 1996 but not in 2005.

Here, for the first time, and for the convenience of American readers, some few further editor's Notes have been added in a section of their own. Finally, I would like to express my gratitude and thanks for the help, support, and advice provided by Sukey Fisher of the Roy Fisher Estate, Neil Astley at Bloodaxe Books, and Devin Johnston at Flood Editions.

P.R.

A FURNACE

INTROIT

12 November 1958

November light low and strong
crossing from the left
finds this archaic
trolleybus, touches the side of it up
into solid yellow and green.

This light is without
rarity, it is an oil,
amber and clear that binds in
this alone and suggests
no other. It is a pressing
medium, steady to a purpose.

And in the sun's ray through the glass
lifting towards low noon, I
am bound;
            boots on the alloy
fenders that edge the deck,

lost out of the day
between two working calls
and planted alone
above the driver's head.
High over the roadway
I'm being swung out
into an unknown crosswise
route to a connection
at the Fighting Cocks
by way of Ettingshall;

old industrial road,
buildings to my left along the flat
wastes between townships
wrapped in the luminous
haze underneath the sun,
their forms cut clear and combined
into the mysteries, their surfaces
soft beyond recognition;

and as if I was made
to be the knifeblade, the light-divider,
to my right the brilliance strikes out perpetually
into the brick house-fields towards Wolverhampton,
their calculable distances
shallow with detail.

*

What is it, this
sensation as of freedom? Tang of
town gas, sulphur, tar,
settled among the heavy
separate houses behind
roadside planes, pale, patch-barked
and almost bare,
the last wide stiffened leaves
in tremor across their shadows
with trolley-standards of green cast iron
reared among them, the catenaries
stretching a net just over my guided head,
its roof of yellow metal.

A deserted, sun-battered theatre
under a tearing sky
is energy, its date 19☐02
spread across its face, mark of
anomaly. And the road
from Bilston to Ettingshall begins
beating in. Whatever
approaches my passive taking-in,
then surrounds me and goes by
will have itself understood only

phase upon phase
by separate involuntary
strokes of my mind, dark
swings of a fan-blade
that keeps a time of its own,
made up from the long
discrete moments
of the stages of the street,
each bred off the last as if by
causality.
                    Because
of the brick theatre struck to the roadside
the shops in the next
street run in a curve, and
because of that there is raised up
with red lead on its girders
a gasworks
close beyond the roofs,

and because of the fold of the
folding in of these three to me
there comes a frame tower with gaps
in its corrugated cladding
and punched out of the sheets high
under its gable
a message in dark empty holes, USE GAS.

*

Something's decided
to narrate
in more dimensions than I can know
the gathering in
and giving out of the world on a slow
pulse, on a metered contraction
that the senses enquire towards
but may not themselves
intercept. All I can tell it by
is the passing trace of it
in a patterned agitation of
a surface that shows only
metaphors. Riddles. Resemblances
that have me in the chute
as it meshes in closer, many modes
funnelling fast through one event,
the flow-through so
dense with association
that its colour comes up, dark
brownish green, soaked and
decomposing leaves
in a liquor.

*

And the biggest of all the apparitions,
the great iron
thing, the ironworks,
reared up on end into the bright
haze, makes quiet burning
if anything at all.

When the pulse-beat for it comes
it is revealed, set
back a little way, arrested,
inward, grotesque, prepared for.

Then gone by,
with the shallowing of the road
and the pulse's falling away
cleanly through a few more
frames of buildings, noise,
a works gate with cyclists;
the passing of it quite final, not a tremor
of the prospect at the crossroads;
open light, green paint on a sign,
the trolley wires
chattering and humming from somewhere else.

I. CALLING

Waiting in blood. Get out of the pit.
That is the sign for parting. Already
the world could be leaving us.

*

Ancient
face-fragments of holy saints
in fused glass, blood-red and blue,
scream and stare and whistle
from where they're cobbled
into a small
new window beside the Dee;
trapped and raving
they pierce the church wall
with acids, glances of fire and lenses out of the light
that wanders under the trees and around
the domed grave-cover
lichened the colour of a duck's egg.

A pick-handle or a boot
long ago freed them

to do these things;
or what was
flung as a stone,
having come slowly on
out of a cloudiness in the sea.

*

Late at night
as the house across the street
stands rigid to the wind
and the lamp on its concrete column plays
static light on to it
everything writhes
through the unstable overgrown philadelphus
covering the whole end wall, its small heart-leaves
flickering into currents that
rock across the wall diagonally upward
and vanish, pursued, white
blossom-packs plucked at hard
and the tall stems
swirled to and fro, awkward
in the floods of expression.

A year or two past the gale
I walk out of the same door

on a night when I have
no depth. Neither
does the opposed house,

the great bush,
glory of the wall, sawn back
for harbouring insurrection and ghosts.

Now nothing
the whole height of the brickwork
to intercept expression.

—You'll know this ten-yard stretch
of suburban tarmac, where something
shakes at you; this
junction-place of back lanes, rutted gullies
with half a car
bedded in half a garage,
this sudden fence-post that breaks step;

the street, the chemist's shop, the lamp;

a stain in the plaster that so
resembles—and that body of air
caught between the ceiling

and the cupboard-top, that's like
nothing that ever was.

*

A tune
is already a metaphor
and a chord
a metaphor wherein
metaphors meet.

*

Wastes of distant darkness
and a different wind
out of the pit
blasts over a desolate
village on the outskirts
after midnight. Driving fast
on peripheral roads
so as to be repeatedly elsewhere
I pick up out of the blackness
waving torches, ahead and
over to one side.

And they are white, and lilac,
lemonade, crimson, magenta,
dull green;

festive little bulbs
strung between poles, left out
to buck and flail, rattling
all night,
        receding as I go,
the last lights,
the only lights.

The sign they make as I pass
is ineluctable
disquiet. Askew. The sign, once there,
bobbing in the world,
rides over intention, something
let through in error.

    *

Sudden and grotesque
callings. Grown man
without right learning; by nobody
guided to the places; not knowing
what might speak; having eased awkwardly
into the way of being called.

    *

In the places,
on their own account, not

for anybody's comfort:
gigantic peace.

Iron walls
tarred black, and discoloured,
towering in the sunlight
of a Sunday morning on
Saltley Viaduct.

Arcanum. Forbidden
open space, marked out with
tramlines in great curves among blue
Rowley Rag paving bricks.

Harsh reek in the air
among the monstrous squat
cylinders puts it
beyond doubt. Not a place
for stopping and spying.

The single human refuge
a roadside urinal, rectangular
roofless sarcophagus of tile and brick,
topped round with spikes and
open to the sky.

*

The few moments in the year when the quadruped
rears on its hindlegs to mount,
foreparts and head
disconnected, hooves dangling,
the horned head visibly not itself;
but something.

*

Waiting in blood.
The sign for parting. The straight way forward
checks, turns back
and sees it has passed through,
some distance back and without knowing it,
the wonderful carcass,
figurehead or spread
portal it was walking,
walking to be within;

showing from a little distance now its
unspeakable girdering, waste cavities,
defenceless structures in collapse; grey
blight of demolition without removal,
pitiable and horrific;

the look that came forward and through
and lit the way in.

    *

Gradbach Hill, long hog's back
stretching down west among taller hills
to the meeting of Dane River
with the Black Brook skirting its steeper side,
the waters joining
by Castor's Bridge, where the bloomery
used to smoke up into the woods
under the green chapel;
the hill,
stretching down west from Goldsitch
a mile from my side yard, shale measures
on its back and the low black spoilheaps
still in the fields,
darkens to an October sunset
as if it were a coal,
the sun sinking into Cheshire, the light
welling up slow along the hillside,
leaving the Black Brook woods
chill, but striking for a while
fire meadows out of red-brown soft-rush,
the dark base, the hollows, the rim swiftly
blackening and crusting over.

II. THE RETURN

Whatever breaks
from stasis, radiance or dark
impending, and slides
directly and fast on its way, twisting
aspect in the torsions of the flow
this way and that,

                then suddenly
over,

    through a single
glance of another force touching it or
bursting out of it sidelong,

doing so
fetches the timeless flux
that cannot help but practise
materialization,
the coming into sense,
to the guesswork of the senses,
the way in cold air
ice-crystals, guessed at, come densely
falling from where they were not;

and it fetches
timeless identities
riding in the flux with no
determined form, cast out of the bodies
that once they were, or out of
the brains that bore them;

but trapped into water-drops,
windows they glanced through
or had their images
detained by and reflected
or into whose molten glass the coloured oxides
burned their qualities;

like dark-finned fish embedded in ice
they have life in them that can be revived.

    *

There is ancient
and there is seeming ancient;
new, and seeming new—
venerable cancer, old as the race,
but so made as to bear
nothing but urgencies—

there is persuading the world's
layers apart with means
that perpetually alter and annex,
and show by the day what they can;

but still, with hardly a change to it,
the other dream or intention: of encoding
something perennial
and entering Nature thereby.

The masque for that
comes in its own best time
but in my place.

Bladelike and eternal, clear,
the entry into Nature
is depicted by
the vanishing of a gentleman
in black, and in portraiture,
being maybe a Doctor John
Dee, or Donne, or Hofmannsthal's
Lord Chandos,
                    he having lately walked
through a door in the air

among the tall
buildings of the Northern Aluminium Company
and become inseparable
from all other things, no longer
capable of being imagined
apart from them, nor yet of being
forgotten in his identity.

All of that is enacted
at the far top
of the field I was born in,

long slope of scrub, then pasture,
still blank on the map three hundred years
after the walkings of all such gentlemen
out of the air

then suddenly printed across with
this century, new, a single
passage of the roller
dealing out streets of terraces
that map like ratchet-strips, their gables
gazing in ranks above the gardens
at a factory sportsground,
a water-tower for steam-cranes, more

worksheds, and,

             hulking along a bank
for a sunset peristyle, the long dark
tunnel-top roof of a football stadium.

All so mild, so late
in that particular change;
still seeming new.

             Some of it,
my streets—Kentish Road,
Belmont, Paddington, Malvern—
just now caught up and lacquered
as Urban Renewal, halted
in the act of tilting to break up
and follow the foundries out
and the stamping mills,
the heavy stuff; short lives, all of them.

But still through that place
to enter Nature; it was possible,
it was imperative.

Something always
coming out, back against the flow,
against the drive to be in,

                              close to the radio,
the school, the government's wars;

the sunlight, old and still,
heavy on dry garden soil,

and nameless mouths,
events without histories, voices,
animist, polytheist, metaphoric,
coming through;

the sense of another world
not past, but primordial,
everything in it
simultaneous, and moving
every way but forward.

Massive in the sunlight, the old woman
dressed almost all in black, sitting out
on a low backyard wall,
rough hands splayed on her sacking apron
with a purseful of change in the pocket,
black headscarf tight across the brow, black
cardigan and rough skirt, thick stockings,
black shoes worn down;

                              this peasant
is English, city born; it's the last
quarter of the twentieth century
up an entryway
in Perry Barr, Birmingham, and there's
mint sprouting in an old
chimneypot. No imaginable
beginning to her epoch, and she's
ignored its end.

    *

Timeless identities,
seeming long
like the one they called Achilles,
or short, like William Fisher,
age ten years, occupation, jeweller,
living in 1861 down Great King Street
in a household
headed by his grandmother, my ancestress
Ann Mason, fifty-seven, widow,
occupation, mangler; come in
from Hornton, back of Edge Hill,
where the masons were quarrying for Christminster.

    *

These identities, recorded by authority
to be miniaturized; to be traceable
however small; to be material;
to have status in the record;
to have the rest,
the unwritten,
even more easily scrapped.

*

Mind
and language
and mind out of language again, and
language again and for ever

fall slack and pat
by defect of nature
into antinomies. Unless

thrown. And again
and repeatedly thrown
to break down the devil
his spirit; to pull down
the devil his grammar school,
wherein the brain
submits to be

cloven, up,
sideways and down
in all of its pathways;

where to convert
one term to its antithesis
requires that there be devised
an agent with authority—

and they're in. That's it. Who
shall own death? Spoken for,
and Lazarus the test case. Only Almighty
God could work that trick. Accept
that the dead have gone away to God through
portals sculpted in brass to deter,
horrific. The signs of it, passably
offensive in a cat or a herring,
in a man are made out
unthinkably appalling: *vide*
M. Valdemar's selfless
demonstration; drawn back and forth,
triumphantly racked in a passage without
extent, province of the agent,
between antithesis and thesis.

Sale and Lease-back. Perennial
wheeze. In the body's exuberance
steal it, whatever it is, sell it back again,
buy it in, cheap,
put it out to rent. If it's freedom, graciously
grant it,
          asking in return no more than
war service, wage-labour, taxes,
custodial schooling, a stitched-up
franchise. Trade
town futures for fields,
railroad food in, sell it on the streets.

And as if it were a military installation
specialize and classify and hide
the life of the dead.

          *

Under that thunderous
humbug they've been persistently
coming and going, by way of
the pass-and-return valve between the worlds,
not strenuous; ghosts
innocent of time, none the worse
for their adventure, nor any better;

that you are dead
turns in the dark of your spiral,
comes close in the first hours after birth,
recedes and recurs often. Nobody
need sell you a death.

*

The ghosts' grown children
mill all day in the Public Search Office
burrowing out names for their own bodies, finding
characters with certificates but no
stories. Genetic behaviour,
scrabbling, feeling back across the spade-cut
for something; the back-flow of the genes'
forward compulsion suddenly
showing broken, leaking out, distressed.

*

They come anyway
to the trench,
the dead in their surprise,
taking whatever form they can
to push across. They've no news.
They infest the brickwork. Kentish Road
almost as soon as it's run up

out in the field, gets propelled
to the trench, the soot still fresh on it,

and the first few dozen faces
take the impress, promiscuously
with door and window arches;
Birmingham voices in the entryways
lay the law down. My surprise
stares into the walls.

III. AUTHORITIES

If only the night can be supposed
unnaturally tall, spectrally
empty, and ready to disgorge
hidden authorities,
summonses, clarifications;

if it can be accorded pomp
to stretch this Grecian office-block
further up into the darkness, lamplit
all the way from the closed shopfronts
and growing heavier; then

that weight of attribution
jolts the entire thing down, partway
through its foundations, one corner heaving
into this panelled basement
where by the bar
the light spreads roseate and dusty.

If all that, then this,
ceiling sagged, drunk eyes

doing the things they do,
stands to be one of the several
cysts of the knowledge, distributed
unevenly through the middle of the mass;
if not, then not.

Brummagem conjuration
for the late Fifties. Not many
hypotheses in play then, even with the great
crust of brick and tarmac finally
starting to split and break up,
the dead weight of the old imperious
racket thrashing on
across its own canted-up wreckage.

Hard to be there, the place
unable to understand
even its own Whig history
for what it was; teachers
trained not to understand it
taught it, and it never fitted. Even less
did the history of the class struggle
reach down or along to the working-
class streets where work and wages
hid, as the most real shame.
      —Don't

ask your little friend
what his father does;
don't let on we've found out
his mother goes to work;
don't tell anyone at all
what your father's job is.
If the teacher asks you
say you don't know.
                    Hard
to be still there. In the razings
and ripping of the slopes, the draining
away of districts, a quick irregular
stink of its creation coming through,
venerable, strong and foul.

    *

Drawn to the places
by their oddness;
guided by nobody
to the subterranean
pea-green cafés,
the cafés in the style of lit
drains, the long plunging
high-walled walkway down
beside the railway viaduct
into moments that would

realign the powers if they could only
be distended;

sent by nobody,
meeting nobody
but the town gods.

The town gods are parodic,
innocent. They've not
created anything. Denizens.
Personages who keep strange hours,
who manifest
but are for the most part mute,

being appearances,
ringed eyes,
ikons designed to stare out
at the ikon-watcher, the studious
artisan walking in wait
at strange hours for the guard
to drop. Haunted
voyeur.

What could they ever say?
Wrecked people

with solitary trajectories,
sometimes rich clothing,
moving against the street currents
or lit from above, standing in bars;
always around the places
where the whores in the afternoon
radiate affront.
                    If this were art
these beings could be
painted into the walls and released
from their patrolling.

    *

In the hierarchies, however disordered,
it would be warlords, kings and those
with the strength to usurp who went, clean,
to the disreputable, undeniable oracle
to have their own thoughts
twisted back in through their ears in style;

in the civilization of novels,
the fields racked hard
to shake people off into suburbs
quiescent with masterless men
in their generations, it would be

pacifist mystics, self-chosen,
who would be driven by private
obsessions to go looking
among slurries and night-holes
for what might be accidentally
there, though not instituted; having to be
each his own charlatan.

*

Grotesquely called,
grotesquely going in, fools
persisting in their folly,
all isolates, supposing
differently, finding differently: priests'
sons with dishevelled wits, teachers
with passed-on clothes and a little Homer,
a little Wordsworth, two or three
generations of Symbolist poets; compelled
by parody to insist
that what image the unnatural
law had been stamping
was moving into Nature,
and, once there,
could not but have its
orifices of question.

*

Sadist-voyeur,
stalled and stricken, fallen
into that way from the conviction of
not doing but
only looking;

nothing to be shot for,
forcibly drugged or even
set about in the free market
and kicked insensible;
invitations to conform, assumptions
of healing, animal sanity, left
to women's initiatives
in the style of the time; teachers
with slipped-off clothes, drawing back
the candlewick covers of the time,
jerking artistically,
letting faith pace observation.

   *

If this were sanity and
sanity were art, this morning street
outside the old music shop would be
robustly done. Portrayal of the common
people and their commonplace bosses
with classless nostalgia. Courbet

transfigured into every substance of it;
every sensation that surrounds,
passes or emanates
entering the world in the manner of
telling or seeing; with no need
to be lifted by art out of
the nondescript general case because never
for a second inhabiting it; detectable
identities, of gear-shifts, stumblings, jackets,
coming through unimpeded.

    *

Birmingham voice
hollow under the dark
arch of the entryway,

by slow torsion wrenched
out of her empty jaw, sunk
hole of lips; no way it could be
understood or answered.

The nearest people. Neighbour-fear
for the children, nine
inches of brick away
year after year from the beginning;

barren couple, the man desperate,
irascible, the woman
namelessly sick, tottering
in extremis for years, bald, spectral,
skin sunk from sallow
to sooty brown, wide eyes set
straight ahead, yellowing,
walking dead. Early

learning. And the dog,
dung-coloured whirl of hatred
too quick for a shape, never still,
slavering and shouting
to hurl itself against the garden
palings repeatedly. A welcome
for my first free steps among the flowers.
Slow-dying woman,
her life was primordial and total,
the gaze-back of the ikon; her death
modern and nothing, a weekend in the Cold War.
The dog must have brained itself.

Had the three of them been art, it would all have
been beaten pewter, dulling
in low relief,

or the grey
sculpture-gibbet of an *enclos paroissial,*
exemplary figures of misery hobbled
to a god bent on confusion,
mercilessly modelled,
glistening when rained on.

His widowhood
was modern and quiet, his death
art: upright in his armchair in the daylight,
facing the door, his eyes
oddly narrowed and suspicious, just
as they were in his life.
He was silvered. It was done.

*

Once invented, the big city
believed it had a brain; Joe
Chamberlain's sense of the corporate
signalling to itself with millions of disposable
identity-cells, summary and tagged.

Right under all that, the whole
construction continued to seethe
and divide itself by natural law; not

into its tributary villages again,
but winning back Dogpool,
Nechells, Adderley Park and the rest

in the cause of a headless
relativity of zones, perceptible
by the perceiver, linked by back roads,

unstable, dividing, grouping again
differently; giving the slip to being
counted, mapped or ever recognized
by more than one head at a time.

Vigilant dreaming head
in search of a place to lay itself.

IV. CORE

Dead acoustic.

Dead space.

Chamber with no echo
sits at the core, its place
plotted by every force. Within,
a dead fall.

Grave goods that have motion
have it on their own account,
respond to nothing.
The chamber whose location knots
an entire symmetry
uses none.

Heterogeneous,
disposed without rhythm,
climax, idiom or generic law,

grave goods send word back out.

*

That sky-trails may merge with earth-trails,
the material spirits
moving in rock as in air,

it's down by just a step or two
into the earth, mounded above at the sky,

and the floor obliquely
tilting a little
to the upper world again.

We're carving the double spiral
into this stone; don't
complicate or deflect us.
We know what we're at.

We're letting the sun perceive
we've got the hang of it.

Write sky-laws into the rocks; draw
the laws of light into it and through it.

On the door under the ground
have them face inwards
into what might otherwise seem dark.

    *

Inside a total stillness
as if inside the world but nowhere
continuous with it,

a warehouse with blocked
windows, brickwork and staging
done matt black
and cleverly lit to resemble
a warehouse
put to night uses;

suspended in there, moving
only on its own account,
the image, *deus mortuus*,
death chuckling along in its life,
uncanny demonstration, one edge
of clowning, charlatan,
the other huskily
brushing against nothing,

in the outermost arm of the spiral,
where it disintegrates,
gives itself up, racing
to flake away,

he is once again passing
close to his birth; Hawkins
on his last go-round,

declining solids, genially
breaking apart, brown man
with papery skin
almost as grey as his
beard and long hair,
the look of a hundred winters
down on his shrunk shoulders

that shake with a mysterious
mutter and chuckle across the mouthpiece,
private, bright-eyed, hung
light in his jacket, shuffling
on wrecked legs,
the old
bellow, the tight leathery sound
shredded, dispersed,

the form of a great force
heard as a monstrously amplified
column of breath, with
scribbles of music across it.

*

Without motion, or sign of motion,
or any history of it,

a polished black basalt
pyramid, household size.

Reflective hornblende faces, wedges
that seem ageless but not old;

here flown as fugitive
from all exegesis.

*

Peachy light
of a misty late afternoon
strokes, with some difficulty
for all they're above ground, the bared
cheekbones of certain villagers;

has to get round
the bulk of St. Fiacre
and through the tall open stone-framed
window-spaces of the modest lean-to
ossuary by the wall;

and has to
pick them out in there
from among shovels, vases,
wheelbarrows, watering-cans;
and go in to them by
their personal windows.

They're on a shelf,
the last half-dozen or so,
up out of the way,

housed in a style
between hatbox and kennel,
tin, or matchwood, painted
black, painted pale green,
skull-patterned,
lettered, *Chef de M.–*,
Chef de Mlle.–, and dated. First
quarter, twentieth century.

    *

Over on Barnenez headland
the long stepped cairn
heavily drawn
across the skyline
has itself seen to be on watch,

powerfully charged
with the persons of certain
translated energies,

the wall of masonry courses
spiked with them, passages,
a bank of ovens in a tilery,
their dispositions
by no means symmetrical;

their buried radiance
variable, heavily shielded,
constantly active; of fearsomely
uncertain mood and
inescapable location.

V. COLOSSUS

The scheme
of Adolphe Sax

that there should be
a giant presence in the sky

rearing above Paris,
slung between four
towers taller than Notre Dame;

blaring into the rain,
a vast steam organ
in the style of the technology and the time,
its truck-sized player-cylinders fed to it
by locomotives;
                    all found in the heart
and its logic, just as Piranesi found
what was appalling but unbuilt.

Le Nôtre, L'Enfant
surfaced closer to the possible.

Paris was spared
the sight of the colossus
rising in a forest of sticks, the way
sections of Liberty in the foundry-yard
towered behind the houses,

and also the inevitable doom of it, cannonaded,
rusted and sagging, enormous
broken image of the Siege.

    *

And up comes the Grand Fleet
from the floor of Scapa Flow,

pale-bellied, featureless, decomposing,
bloated with pumped air,

breaking the grey surface, hulk after hulk,
huge weight of useful iron

slithered across, cut into,
sold off: worn tanks of fire

that trundled through the sea,
both sides' dirty coal-smoke
blown the same way in battle.

*

Clarity
of the unmoving core
comes implacably out
through all that's material:

walls of battleship scrap,
the raising up of Consett
along the skyline,
the taking of it down again.

*

Mansions of manufacturers strung along ridges
upwind of prosperity built in infernal
images below,
                   well out of it, but not yet
out of sight.
                   Were they
mansions in Paradise, looking out over Hell?
Were they mansions in the better parts of Hell?

Question evaded by the model
chief residences of the model factories,
set upon slight
elevations of the Middle Way.

*

This age has a cold blackness of Hell
in cities at night. London
is filled with it, Chicago cradles it
in ice-green glitter along
the dark of the lake. Birmingham Sparkbrook,
Birmingham centre, Birmingham Castle Vale
hang in it as holograms. For now

Puritan materialism dissolves its matter,
its curdled massy acquisition; dissolves
the old gravity of ponderous fires
that bewildered the senses,
                                                    and for this
glassy metaphysical void.

Something will be supposed
to inhabit it, though it is not
earth, sky or sea. There will be
spastic entrepreneurial voyages twitched out
from wherever its shores may lie.

*

Mercurial nature with a heaviness to it
flies with an eye to sitting
down somewhere and being serious.

With a heaviness to it, an opacity
saddening its flight.

Haunted look of stalled energy, of rights
impatiently or contemptuously surrendered.

VI. THE MANY

Transit of Augusta Treverorum
to Trier; a location
busy with evolutionary forms long
before the brain-birth of 1818.

First, a grid-city, fit to support Constantine's
huge palace and basilica, working
as it was designed to do, its defences
anchored to bastions;
the size and operation
generating the structures of the first rank.

The size vanished; the operation
ceased. On all sides
the general case
collapsed, and the nettles grew out of it,

and the beasts fed there and let fall
their dung. There will have been scrub,

and mounds, and the rest of the new
general case of reversion,

out of which still rose up
spaced widely and without relation, certain
of the great masonry contraptions
that gave no proper
account of how they'd been arrived at.

Next, the shelter of each of those things
generated a settlement of scufflers,
scratchers of livings. Pragmatic
tracks linked one with another; in due time
the separate nuclei touched their
forces together and fused

to a mediaeval city which, conceived,
closed off. It walled what it was. It sat

smaller than the Roman city, quite
differently shaped
and oriented; entirely grown
out of the landmarks of that city,
and ignorant of it.

I see such things worked rapidly,
in my lifetime; hard for the body to believe in.

                *

Mercurial nature, travelling fast,
laterally in broken directions, shallow,
spinning, streaked out in separate lights, an
oil film dashed on a ripple,
its plural bands
drawn out and tonguing back on themselves,

in an instant is gone
vertically on a plunge, on a sudden
switch of attitude,
                    without ever
pausing to drop its flight,
compose itself, gain weight;
                               dives
narrowly deep, as far down
as anything;
                    plunges unaltered,
slips away down
in twisted filaments, separable
argumentative lights.

*

Parable of the One and the Many. Presences
flaring out from the wet flints
at Knowlton ruin,

multiple as beans, too small and irregular
to distinguish or call names. Divide;
survive.
     Some god, isolated
by a miscalculation, cut off
from his fellows, hauled in
across the bank to clear the green
ring of its demons; churched over;
and in his time forsaken.

They ate him,
and drank him,
and put his little light out and left.

*

The stones are waters
the stones are fires
dragged in a swirl across the core,

these slopes their after-image
fixed into the longest
fade they can secure;

ice, and sunlight, and blackened
crusts, lichen and heather sweeps
tilting off, one through another.

Draining through peat-hags,
Dane River, by its weight sucked out
from a mile of upland bog

to pour down, stained
through a crumbling, matt-black, moist
ravine of soft, firm

stuff that could be fire;
peat scattered with coal glitter,
mineshafts in a trail before

the drop into pastures.
These moorlands
hang down in swags from the sky,

from graves in the sky,
companies of lives lifted up;
Stanton Moor, Knot Low,

Shutlingsloe,
tilted, eroded cone,
mutable, as the lands turn on it,

as if it were a cloud shape
or the massing of a mood, emerging
to be directly read.

Over away from Dane
Axe Edge sends down the Dove,
gathers the Manifold

and lets it slip
through complexity;
the hills in their turns tantalize

and instruct, then the learning
dissolves. There's no
holding it all. Steadily

as the star-fields swing by,
this land-maze
brushes against, and stirs

somnolent body-tracks, unmapped
traces in the brain.
Axe Edge

thrust up towards the anvil-cloud
full of rivers, the skyline
inky and dark. Under

the evening, the hoof-strike flashes.

*

Landscape superimposed
upon landscape. The method
of the message lost
in the poetry of Atlantis
at its subsiding to where all
landscapes must needs be
superimpositions on it. All landscapes
solid, and having transparency
in time, in state. Odysseus old—
what to do with him?

—sent out to have his hardened
senses touch against lost reality.
It is called water that he passes through.

*

The boys are swinging firecans
along through the dusk;

rusty cans, bodged with holes,
with long string handles, coals from the grate

and whistled through oxygen to make
red-eyed pepperpots, clustered

fire-points, raging away in a trail
of acrid chimney smoke in the street.

*

The land, high and low,
has been scattered across with fire-pots;
brick, iron, lidded, open to the sky,
the glare streaming upward
in currents and eddies of sparks, blackening
the look of the rim, the district,
even by day, requiring that it be
strong; that it shall one day split itself.

*

The true gods, known only
as *those of whom there is never news*;

rebellious, repressed; indestructible
right access to the powers of the world;

by tyrannies given images; given
finish, given work; and in due time

discarded among the débris of that into
private existences, into common use,

deliquescent, advancing by a contrary
evolution to the giving up of all

portrayable identity, seeping unevenly
down to a living

level, pragmatic
skein of connections from

lichens to collapsing faces
in drenched walls, exhalations

of polish and detergent
in palace-voids of authority,

patches of serene light in the skulls of
charlatans making tea in swamp cottages,

evidences that dart into the particle accelerator
unaccountably; and others

caught unawares in the promiscuous
rectangles of the Impressionists,

and ready to come back out to us
through the annexation-frames
of a world that thought itself a single colony.

*

Coming home by the road across Blackshaw Moor
in a summer dawn with the ridge just showing
grey above the plain and out of the white mist;

a red eye goggling high in the dark rocky
crest of Hen Cloud, a lamp in crimson canvas
up there somewhere. That skyline
was mad enough already.

*

One particular of Poseidon: the bronze statue
through whose emptied eyeholes
entire Poseidon comes and goes.

VII. ON FENNEL-STALKS

They have no choice but to appear.

We knew they existed, but not what they'd be like;
this visitation is the form that whatever
has been expected but not imaged takes
for the minutes it occupies now.

                                    Just after sunset,
looking out over the thin snow,
the moor vegetation, stiff canopy,
showing through it, greying. Wind
getting up, dragging smoky cloud-wisps
rapidly across on a line
low in the sky.

                Another wind,
steady and slow from the north, freezing
and far higher; and with it,
rising from behind the ridge, gigantic
heads lifted and processing along it, sunset-lit,
five towering beings
looking to be miles high,

their lower parts hidden, their lineaments
almost stable in their infinitely slow
movement.
        Relief at the sight of them
even though they seem to mean
irrevocable dislocation. Creatures
of the Last Days, coming to the muster.

Apocalypse
lies within time; as these beings
may or may not so lie; if they do,
their demeanour could equally match
the beginning of all things. It's the same
change. There's a choice of how to see it.

For them, no such choice. Self-generated,
and living perfect to themselves
in some other dimension, they have it
laid on them to materialize in the cold
upper air of the planet;
and arriving there
they can take on only the shapes
the terms of materialization impose.

Visibly not as they would wish to be,
they're self-absorbed. The human eye

watches them shrewdly, albeit
with the awe it's been craving; sizes them up,
how to ride them.

    *

Cargo-cult
reversed. There have always been
saucers put out for us
by the gods. We're called
for what we carry.

In barbarous times
all such callings
come through as rank parodies,

refracted by whatever murk
hangs in the air;
even the long pure
sweep of the English pastoral
that stretched its heart-curve
stronger, and more remarkably wide

merely to by-pass
the obstruction caused by a burst
god, the spillage

staining the economic imperative
from end to end with divinity.

＊

Mythos,
child of action, mother of action;

hunger for action understands itself
only by way of its own

secretion, fluid metaphysical carrier
that makes, where it collides, cultures,

and where it runs free, myth,
child of action, mother of action.

＊

There can be quaint cultures
where a poet who incurs exile
will taste it first,
                    puzzling half a life
at the statues in the town park and those
particular shin-high railings there;

afterwards, fame and disgrace.

Succeeding a single blink of passage
through a beam of power
on the road between fortunes; between
province and metropolis,
art and art, fantasy
and amenity.

    *

The snails of Ampurias
ascend
       as the canopy of air
upon the ruins
cools after sunset.

They infest
       the wild fennel
that infests the verges of the road
through what have become wide
spaces above the bay.

The snails ascend
       the thin clear light,
taking their spirals higher;
       in the dusk
luminous white, clustered
like seed-pods of some other plant;

quietly

rasping their way round

                together, and upward;

tight and seraphic.

Appendix

THEY COME HOME

To win back the parents
from the passage-laws;
bring them home together,
bury them under a tree;

spread their bone-dust,
that now stares back at the sun
for the first time and not for long,
two colours of dry limestone,
female and male,
met for the first time, your
fingers and mine mixing your dead
in a layer across the topsoil,
set with corms,
aconite and crocus,
directly under a double-winged
trapdoor of live turf;

by no means separate the dead
from anything.

To have them
won back, by awkward custom;
lifted free
of the crematorium counter
and out from the poor
vestige of common ceremony;

left to our own devices, holding them,
each in a stout paper bag that
covers a squarefaced container
of dull plastic, coloured like
milky cocoa, with a toning beige lid.

And the last journey of all, of necessity
by way of the car-exhaust workshop;

they travel, your foot steadying them upright,
together on the floor, concentrated,
come down to owl-size in their jars,

and they stay there for an hour without us,
lifted up high on the greased, shining
hydraulic pillars under the workshop roof-lights,
closed in my grey-green car

while its rusted and burnt-out piping gets
yanked off and replaced. They come home
over a new smell of hot metal.

By no means separate
from anything at all.

Jars and their paper bags,
name-labels,
go to the bin, with the clearings-out
from the discontinued kitchen;

each has still
a whisper of human dust that
clings to the plastic,
the boundary a mad
regress beyond the microscopic.

They're going again in a day or two:

to be in part twice-burned
in city flames; eight hundred
degrees of the lance-burner

under the oven's
brick arch, and then whatever
blast of the municipality
lifts the remainder haze clear of Sheffield
and over the North Sea.

Preface

A Furnace is an engine devised, like a cauldron, or a still, or a blast-furnace, to invoke and assist natural processes of change; to persuade obstinate substances to alter their condition and show relativities which would otherwise remain hidden by their concreteness; its fire is Heraclitean, and will not give off much Gothic smoke.

Some of the substances fed in are very solid indeed: precipitates, not only topographical, of industrial culture in its rapid and heavy onset, when it bred a new kind of city whose images dominated people's intelligences in ways previously unknown.

The poem is also an homage, from a temperament very different from his, to the profound, heterodox and consistent vision of John Cowper Powys, to whom I owe thanks for some words of exhortation he gave me in my youth and in his old age. More importantly, I am indebted to his writings for such understanding as I have of the idea that the making of all kinds of identities is a primary impulse which the cosmos itself has; and that those identities and that impulse can be acknowledged only by some form or other of poetic imagination. There is also, in his novel *Atlantis*, a description of a lost poem which gains its effects by the superimposition of landscape upon landscape rather than rhythm upon rhythm; without having that idea as a scheme I have, indeed, set one landscape to work with another in this poem, more by way of superimposition than comparison: Birmingham, where I was born in a district that had not long since been annexed from the southern edge of the old county of Staffordshire, and the stretch of hill country around the northern tip of the same county where I have been living recently; about the same size as Birmingham, and, in its way, equally complex.

A Furnace is a poem containing a certain amount of history, and the sequence of its movements is based on a form which enacts, for me, the equivocal nature of the ways in which time can be thought about. This is the ancient figure of the double spiral, whose line turns back on itself at the centre and leads out again, against its own incoming curve. After the 'Introit', which identifies the poem's preoccupations in the sort of setting in which they were forcing themselves on me at the time I wrote the pieces which were to be published as *City* in 1961, the seven movements proceed as if by a section taken through the core of such a spiral, with the odd-numbered ones thematically touched by one direction of the spiral's progress, and the even-numbered so touched by its other, returning, aspect; the exception is the fourth section, which is at the centre and thus has the theme of stillness.

Author's Notes

14: *Gradbach Hill.* In North-West Staffordshire close to Three Shires Head, where Derbyshire, Cheshire, and Staffordshire meet. Facing it across the Black Brook is the rocky cleft called Lud's Church, a place whose supposed connection with the composition of *Sir Gawain and the Green Knight* I am willing to believe in.

16: *Like dark-skinned fish* . . . etc. Quoted from J. C. Powys, *Maiden Castle* (Macdonald, 1937).

23: *M. Valdemar.* Suspended for months on end in the moment of death, in Poe's story.

43: *Barnenez.* Ancient tumulus on the Kernéléhen peninsula in Brittany, no great distance from the village of St. Fiacre.

46: The German Grand Fleet surrendered at Scapa Flow after the First World War, and was then scuttled by its crews. Pictures of the raising of the ships were some of the most awesome images I saw in childhood.

50: *The brain-birth of 1818.* The brain was Karl Marx's.

53: *Knowlton.* In Dorset. An abandoned Christian church stands in the ring of an enclosure previously sacred to earlier deities whose ground it was tactically sent to occupy.

55: *Axe Edge.* In Derbyshire, and reaching down to Three Shires Head (q.v.). Within a mile or so of one another, on or under Axe Edge, rise three rivers: the Dane, flowing west into Cheshire, the Dove, flowing east, and the Manifold, running close to the Dove and eventually joining it.

59: *Blackshaw Moor, Hen Cloud.* An upland plain in North-West Staffordshire, and a crag overlooking it.

65: *Ampurias.* Extensive Celtiberian, and later Roman, mercantile settlement in Catalonia.

Notes

2-3: *Fighting Cocks, Ettingshall,* and *Bilston.* Cock fighting was a popular West-Midlands sport and so a common pub name. Ettingshall and Bilston are areas around Wolverhampton.

7: The river *Dee* referred to here is the one in Cheshire that flows out into the Irish Sea on the western side of the Wirral peninsula.

12: *Saltley Viaduct* marks the entrance to this densely populated inner-city area of Birmingham.

12: *Rowley Rag paving bricks* are made from a distinctive volcanic stone quarried on the west edge of the Black Country, not far from 'The Burning Graves at Netherton' evoked in Fisher's poem of that name.

14: *Castor's Bridge* is a narrow pedestrian walkway across the *Black Brook* near Gradbach and Lud's Church in Derbyshire.

17: *John Dee* (1527-1608) was an occult philosopher and advisor to Queen Elizabeth I. *John Donne* (1572-1631) was a poet and Dean of St Paul's Cathedral. *Hofmannsthal's Lord Chandos* refers to 'The Letter of Lord Chandos', a prose work cast as a missive dated August 1603 from the imaginary Philip, Lord Chandos, to Francis Bacon, in which he reports a crisis of creativity and language. The Austrian writer Hugo von Hofmannsthal (1874-1929) composed it in 1902.

18: *Northern Aluminium Company,* a British subsidiary of the Canadian parent, now called Alcan, acquired an interest in a foundry in the West Bromwich area of Birmingham in 1926. It produced materials for the construction of Spitfires during World War II.

19: *Kentish Road, Belmont, Paddington, Malvern* are streets in Birmingham. Roy Fisher was born at 74 Kentish Road on 11 June 1930. The other three street names are those of neighbouring roads in this small, contemporaneously built grid close to the borders of Handsworth, West Bromwich, and Smethwick.

21: *Perry Barr* is the next place around the outer circle bus route from Handsworth in Birmingham.

21: *William Fisher* (1826-70) was an electroplater who died young of lung disease, leaving in Great King Street (in the Birmingham jewellery quarter) his widow, Georgina Mason (1828-1919), and a large family. *Ann Mason*, Georgina's widowed mother, was born in 1804 in Oxfordshire, but her death date, most probably between 1861 and 1871, is not known. The following three place names, *Hornton, Edge Hill, Christminster*, are connected with Oxford and Oxfordshire, the first a village in the north of the county and the second also the name of the first battle in the Civil War, which took place on 23 October 1642. The poet's ancestry can be traced back to villages in the vicinity of its battlefield. *Christminster* is the name Thomas Hardy gave to Oxford, figuring most decisively in his 1895 novel *Jude the Obscure*.

25: *Public Search Office* may be a variant name for what is now called The Public Records Office.

28: *Brummagem* is a cant word for Birmingham, originally used to imply showy but shoddy workmanship from a lower level of the traditional manufacturing in the area. The poet's father, Walter Fisher Jr. (1889-1959), was a fine craftsman jeweller and so not a part of this ersatz tier.

28: *Whig history*, treated with some skepticism in *A Furnace*, presents the past as an inevitable progress towards ever greater liberty and enlightenment, leading into contemporary liberal democracy and constitutional monarchy.

36: *Joe Chamberlain* (1836-1914) was an industrialist and Liberal politician, later prime minister, who was decisive in Birmingham's nineteenth-century municipal development. The poet's grandfather Edward Jones (1862-1946) worked for a time as the gardener for his eldest son Austen, also a politician.

37: *Dogpool, Nechells, Adderley Park* are places in inner east Birmingham in the direction of the river Tame's course.

41: Coleman *Hawkins* (1904-69) was an American jazz tenor saxophonist. Fisher saw Hawkins perform at the Opposite Lock Club in Birmingham, a few months before the saxophonist died.

45: *Adolphe Sax* (1814-94) was the Belgian inventor of the saxophone.

45: Giovanni Battista *Piranesi* (1720-78) was an Italian artist famous for his etchings of Roman ruins and invented 'prison' interiors.

45: André *Le Nôtre* (1613-1700) was Louis XIV's principal gardener, and responsible for those at the Palace of Versailles.

45: Peter Charles *L'Enfant* (1754–1825) was a French-born engineer who designed the 'L'Enfant Plan' (1791) for Washington, DC.

46: *Liberty* is the Statue of Liberty, which was transported to New York from Paris, where it had been constructed, emerging between the houses as described in the poem, and arriving in the USA on 17 June 1885.

46: *Siege* is the Siege of Paris (1870–71) in the Franco-Prussian War.

56: *Landscape superimposed / upon landscape* is drawn from the passage concerning an imaginary 'long poem about the beginning and end of everything' where 'the fact that it is landscape superimposed on landscape rather than rhythm upon rhythm is the method of its message' in John Cowper Powys, *Atlantis* (London: MacDonald, 1954), p. 336.

60: *Poseidon* is the Greek god of the sea, earthquakes, soil, storms, and of horses. The *bronze statue* is one recovered off Cape Artemision, in northern Euboea, and now in the National Archaeological Museum of Athens.